Weight Loss for Lovers
Finding my Soul ~~Mate~~ Food

Melissa Templeman

Copyright © 2015 by Melissa Templeman

Weight Loss for Lovers
Finding my Soul Mate Food
by Melissa Templeman

Printed in the United States of America.

ISBN 9781498457583

All rights reserved solely by the author. The author guarantees all contents are original and do not infringe upon the legal rights of any other person or work. No part of this book may be reproduced in any form without the permission of the author. The views expressed in this book are not necessarily those of the publisher.

www.xulonpress.com

ACKNOWLEDGMENTS

As I sit here thinking about all the people in my life (my circle), that helped me along the way. First I would like to thank the TRUE BREAD, that Created My PLATE. As you know it started with the Original, a piece of Spicy and I can't forget my Pumpkin Seeds, I can't wait for a scoop of Pasta, and I will not forget my GREENES, Hey where is my Portion Control? Okay, thank you for serving (you are soooooooo needed). All right then, as I look down at my plate something missing? I'm sorry I have to have my SALT. Last but not least, Dessert, a piece of whipped pie (yum). No more wine for me, but I have to have a tall glass of WATER from Waldorf (it's a Special FLAVOR)Okay now I can eat! Wait, Wait, Oh there you are, here comes BLESSING thank you HONEY.

P.S. I LOVE YOU ALL ####never hungry................

TABLE OF CONTENTS

CHAPTER 1: MOMMY I'M FULL 9

CHAPTER 2: THAT JUST BABY FAT!......................... 11

CHAPTER 3: SOMETHING NEW?.............................13

CHAPTER 4: I'M SERIOUS THIS TIME! 15

CHAPTER 5: SEXY AND I KNOW IT!..........................17

CHAPTER 6: ON MY OWN?...................................21

CHAPTER 7: CHURCHES CHICKEN? 23

CHAPTER 8: GREYGOOSE 25

CHAPTER 9: I MEET ALLWAYS! 27

CHAPTER 10: NOW I'M ADDICTED TO ALWAYS. 29

Chapter 1

MOMMY I'M FULL

Come on brother. Put your bike away it's time to eat! I can't wait, mom is fixing our favorite Chicken and whatever else she's having with it, I hope it's not BEETS, I hate those things. Hey maybe that's her favorite. That's just not right putting Her favorite thing on us, that's just isn't fair. So now for me to get seconds I have to Eat two helpings of BEETS to get more CHICKEN, YUM that's what I'll do. I don't care if I've had enough or not, I'll do whatever it takes to get that CHICKEN! Slow down there's more where that came from, thanks mom one more plate for the road. Come here doggy, why are you not eating those BEETS? Oh No here comes mom, pick up those BEETS off the floor before she yells at us. Go in the bathroom to throw them up, wait then I'll throw up the Chicken also, I do not want to do that, even though I'm full. I wish she would just give me another piece of Chicken instead of me eating two full plates of everything. Maybe she's trying to teach me a lesson? But what? Is it that two plates of food is the norm? I think most parents like it when their children eat all their food and want seconds and not looking at the cost of emotions, reality and control. Now I know why we didn't go out often, because she didn't want to get embarrassed when we asked for seconds, or we would get the **EYE** which tells us you better not look like your gonna ask for another. Next time Mom, tell us that is your LOVE language, that you love to cook and feeding your family, that's what make you happy, when you see a clean plate not two. I know I'm going outside to work off those two slices of bread, but as I get older I would rather watch T.V. and go to sleep, or just eat some more out of boredom. People won't notice I have no control of my eating or maybe they have their own weight issues that they are covering up? WAIT! Am I hungry or WHAT! MOM WHAT'S A PORTION?

Chapter 2

THAT JUST BABY FAT!

Hi, Hey what's up?(me) What's your name? They call me Black Forest Ham. What's your name? I'm Salad. (He don't need to know my real name (Chicken) I mean 3 piece. Hey do you want to go on a date? Sure, let's go out to eat. Okay. (little does he know I will eat before he picks me up, and all I'm going to order is salad). He doesn't know that I'm GREEDY and STARVING for ATTENTION. He doesn't know a couple more meals and he will get all this 3 Piece. Well goodnight, thanks for dinner. Can I have a kiss? No what kind of salad you think I am a leg and thigh? Okay Okay, I'll call you later. May I was being mean I should have kissed him. He probably won't call. I'm hungry! RING……Ring…….. Hey I was thinking about you, and I was thinking about you too! How about a dinner and a movie? Okay. When? Okay great, talk to you later. (Little does he know my stomach is going to growl at the movie, I'm going to have to have something more that a salad for dinner), and maybe if I give him a kiss when he pick me up then he won't notice the full plate I will order or maybe I suggest a buffet. So then I'm killing two birds with one stone…….Months later, WHAT! OH MY GOODNESS, I'M WHAT? PREGNANT! This Salad isn't SEASONED enough for a baby. I'm hungry! RING………RING……. Hey what's up?(me) We need to talk. Okay. I'm Pregnant…Oh. Oh okay I will rob and steel to get pampers and milk. (Now that's LOVE!) What did I just say? I think that was my Breast talking. I never had BLACK Forest before, my mom didn't warn me of the dangers of DARK MEAT. Ouch! What did you hit me for? I have to support a child with no money and no job!(me) Well, how did you take me out to all those dinners? I borrowed it,(That's impressive!)(Did he know he just hit a SALAD or all he saw was a **leg** and a **thigh?** Now I'm really hungry!(Do he know every time he hits me I eat more) .Food you are so Faithful, I love you. So..... Now, I just don't care, because now I can't feel the PAIN of Emotions and the Physical. RING.......RING.......Hello. Hello is Black Forest home (I'm thinking please take him out of here!) Yeah hold on, hey what's up, yeah I'm on the way. Hang up.....So where are you going, I'm going to look for some money! What he really means is he's going to get some drugs to escape his pain. I didn't know you gain a lot of weight when feeding on Black Forest Ham. When someone is feeding you Negativity, Discouragement, Doubt, Lies and their Pain it's Heavy. Whew! That's was close...... Now I'm starting to add BEER with my 3 piece. This is too much! I have a baby now, he keeps crying, let me give him something to eat and me too! YYYYEEEESSSS COMFORT! RING.....RING.....RING.....Hello, hey mom can I come back home to two plates. Yes. Maybe we get back to walking and lose that baby weight. It should have been gone by now right?(She doesn't know I added BEER to me MEAL.) (She doesn't know that I've been Chicken for so long I've turned into a Drunken Pig)! KNOCK............KNOCK.....I'm home, me and baby. LET'S GET WALKING!

Chapter 3
SOMETHING NEW?

Hi………Hi….What's your name? My name is BLACK BULL. Okay….My name is 3piece plus 6 pack and also baby fat. Are you married? (He said) Yes, but I'm separated,(he doesn't know some leftover Black Forest is still in me)). Are You? Yes, but I'm not happy, my wife is always eating. I can't CONTROL her so she eats. (He didn't say that). I was thinking it. So why don't you leave her if your unhappy? Well we have 4 kids and I have to watch what they eat!(me) Well I guess we can see each other on weekends and get to know each other. Months Later……RING…Ring…… He says, Hello , Yeah my wife left me and she took the kids (YES)! YES I get to have him all to myself, she must be crazy to leave this Black Bull or maybe she was tired of all that BULL. I will drink to that. Hello… Yes I'm here, you want to move in? You and baby fat of course. Okay it is closed to my job and he likes to drink with his meal too! Hey..I'm home… are you hungry? No I'd rather Drink my dinner (he didn't say that, but that's what he did). What happened? You look like you're mad at the world. My wife called me and wants money for Her four kids. (HUH?)Well she left me! (Now I see why). So he asked, did you go to the gym today? Yes, I replied. I bought you something. What is it? It's a plastic sweat suit. You start to sweat as soon as you put it on (GEE THANKS!) What was he really trying to say? Don't GAIN any weight? But I have you now, can I let you see the real me? I just want to be LOVED…..You know something about my NEW BULL reminds me of BLACK FOREST. I just can't put my finger on it. Is it that they both are **DARK**? Like a chicken I'm afraid of the **DARK.** Time to go back home to two plates. RING……….RING….Hey mom it's me. You know this time I only added on a little bull with my 3 piece and baby fat. She says, Hey you look fine, thanks mom (that's because she doesn't see the DEPRESSION and ANXIOTY of the MENTAL WEIGHT) My head is Heavy. I got it! I just haven't found the RIGHT MAN. Mom, did you cook? YYYYEEESSS. GOD is GREAT and GOD is GOOD, Thank you for this FOOD! That's got to be the best PRAYER in the world. YUM! Smothered Pork Chops another favorite. She says, Stop eating so fast it's not going anywhere. WHEW, I am FULL that second plate did it, I'm going to lay down…. Ouch! (I'm awake) my head hurts. Why is my head hurting, could it be the food? No WAY! The BEER? The lack of sleep? I am so used to someone Controlling me I don't have SELF CONTROL. What's that? The baby is crying, I know she did not give him pork chops, is she trying to kill him. I'm going to be glad when he is old enough to get me a BEER and fix my plate, while I lay in bed. When is Mothers Day! I'm Hungry.MOM, did you feed him? Can you watch him while I sleep? Don't put the Food up, okay!

Chapter 4

I'M SERIOUS THIS TIME!

ALRIGHT! ALRIGHT! ALREADY! It's time for us to have a talk (FOOD). I don't know why we keep having this same conversation, but different times in my life. I'm tired of you keep Attaching yourself to me, I thought you were my friend and I love you, but sometimes I Love you too much and it's not HEALTHY. All I'm trying to do is LOOK for LOVE the REAL LOVE. And by you keep Creeping back and forth into my life. I think sometimes that you LIE to me, so I can Feel good at the Time. Maybe I should stop going Cold Turkey and take my time and go through the PROCESS. You know maybe I should put the fork down and really listen to my body and not you. I think it's time to break up this cycle of ABUSE. Don't give me that! It's not your routine, we are both Contributing to the Madness, and don't go blaming BEER, don't be quick to blame others for your mistakes. I'm tired of being a Chicken, It's time for me to grow up and take responsibility for my actions. FOOD is Talking, That's fine, but you will be back, because there is no other Love (LUST) out there! Now can I have a kiss goodbye or give it to me when you get back from your so called journey and bring a friend.

Chapter 5

SEXY AND I KNOW IT!

Hi!.........Hi……I've seen you before, do you live around here? No, this is where the Dark Meat hang out. Oh okay, so what's your name (here we go again). My name is six pack and baby fat. What's your name? They call me Candy Corn. HUM? That's different. I think I like him already we are totally opposite, and you know what they say opposites attract. By me drinking BEER I don't have a sweet tooth, that still doesn't make it right.(Should I tell him that BEER enhances my LOVE drive) Nope, he will see. (BEER stop interrupting! I will talk with you later). Do you want to see a movie? Sure, love too. Good I will eat before I go (I miss my friend) I can't go back, I won't, FOOD you are a LIER! Oh No! I feel anxiety coming back, thoughts of another Bad relationship, thoughts of Time wasted. At least I know COMFORT is waiting for me, He is so FAITHFUL. HI. Let's get something to eat, okay, wow, I haven't been to so many restaurants in my life. I love this Candy Corn, but he is too sweet to be true. I can get used to this! I'll drink to that! Months Later……………..(Me talking), I lost my job as I tell Candy Corn. That's okay I'm in pharmaceuticals and I sell Herbs, so we will be okay. Let me try those Herbs you sell. Wow, that's an experience! Hey I'm more hungry than ever, I can eat you, Black Forest, Black Bull and a six pack no twelve. Wait! I can't tell him I eat like that. He will leave me. Oh well I'm just hungry. And I need my **Comfor**t, because **He** is going to be there **ALLWAYS.**

Hey, He is hungry too! He won't even notice that I'm just going along with the program, maybe this is his norm. He sure does eat out a lot (I mean WE). Let's move in together? Okay…..(Yes, again leaving two plates) Yes, mom I'm moving out again, I will make this work by any means! Mom he loves me for the Chicken I am! Don't keep taking baby fat from place to place feeding him everything. I don't want to confuse him,(but Candy loves him too!). We will be alright. Love you. Love you Too! Months later………What I'm Pregnant! YES, more buffets AAWWW! No BEER, that's okay, I have my friend back, now I have an excuse for being overweight. Can't wait to tell Candy Corn! He be glad, because I don't think he wants me to work (another plus) right? Year later…….Now I have two baby fats. Well, I'm glad I can get back to drinking. Yeah there is nothing to do all day is watch soap operas and fix three meals a day, What a life? Right? Glad one baby fat is in school now. Wait! It's time for my SOAPS, I'm glad they can fill my mind with negativity and lust and just plain old Drama. Question? How do they stay so slim? I see them drinking and smoking cigarettes and also eating all these exotic restaurants. I want to be just like them, except for the smoking. You know I think I need a job, who will hire me with these extra pounds on my back, am I waiting for it to knock at my door? Should I tell Candy Corn I want out of this house? I better not he is going to think it's him, maybe I'll tell him over dinner or over some Herbs. Hi…….I'm glad you home, I want to talk about me getting a job. Hey! I take care of you! I know I know, but listen, I want to make my own money. You can't make it without me. I'm not saying I want to leave you, I'm saying I need a job. I'm tired of eating up Loneliness and Depression, maybe he like his Chicken on Steroids. I can't be out of breath just by talking. Months Later……I'm off to work. Whoa, they want me to work every day? I think I'll just work part time for now. I had been home for so long, now I need rehab to walk and talk without being out of breath. Months Later…….I like this job it's flexible, and now I'm working five days a week. The weight is slowly coming off. Months later……I think I've lost 30lbs. YYYEEESSS, maybe because I cut out the Herbs and drinking only a 6pack instead of 12. YYEESS! I can do this, I don't know something inside of me says that, you know let me stop talking to myself, and people will think I'm crazy! Candy Corn is home…..he wants to go out to a buffet (why is he doing that?), do he know I'm trying to lose weight? Does he want me to lose? Does he like steroid Chicken? Does he think if I lose the weight, someone else would want me? Will I want them? Maybe I should ask him, do he want to join me on my journey? Am I thinking of all this stuff? He only asked me: do I want to go to the buffet. Yes, let's go. Let me see if I can Control myself on the outside. NOPE..........I NEED HELP! I do it every time. Trying to do it on my own. Does anybody care that I need help? Now I'm mad at myself and Candy Corn, because it's all his fault, that I can't lose the weight or at least the fatty part of this thigh. How dare he love all this unhealthy weight.....YEARS LATER................10 to be exact, Yes 10 years that came and went. Food, do we need to talk again? It seems I get better results when I talk to myself. Am I talking to myself?

Chapter 6

ON MY OWN?

WOW! I finally got my own place, me and my 2 chickadees. So why I'm not feeling so happy? Is this is the first time I'm alone? For the first time, I'm not running back to two plates. Even though she will welcome me, but I can't keep asking her to take some of the weight off me. I know she will, I need to take charge! HELP...............!!!!!!!!!!!!!! I **WILL HELP YOU**! Who said that? Wait a minute, all this time I've been talking to myself and it really wasn't me? **GOD** is that you? **YES! Every time you was alone and quiet, I was talking to you, but you seemed to only listen when you fail at your own accomplishments. I've been trying to talk to you for years, but you let others Control, Navigate your Emotions. I don't like to see you cry my child. If you keep seeking me, I will lead you, guide you, I have already completed your life. TRUST ME. FEED off ME, I WILL KEEP YOU SATISFIED!**

Chapter 7

CHURCHES CHICKEN?

Okay LORD, I've lost that Ham, that Bull and Candy, now it's just me and you. I feel so much better now, I'm on my own with my two kids, I'm healthy I'm in Church. Now all I need is a husband, so LORD send me a husband ASAP! You know it's been four years since I had a drink, so I'm ready for all you have for me. HELLO……….(Friend calling) Hey girl you want to go to a cookout?(me) Yeah I haven't been out in a while. Later at the cookout……………Hi! (Him) Hi. He said I know your name it's Church, why yes it is, what's your name Seagrams (I was thinking you look like a tall drink!). Can I call you sometime?(me) Sure! Thank you LORD that was quick! This must be my Husband! YES!(me) Do you go to Church? Yeah, I go to my sisters church (found out later that his sister and I attend the same church)YYEEESSSS! This has got to be the one. Thanks GOD I'll take from Here! Weeks later…….moves in with me! YYEESSS! He is helping with the bills. I'm glad he only drinks in the house and not out there drinking and driving. I don't like to time he comes in from work, he wants me to eat dinner with him at 9:00pm and talk about his day. (what about me?) Any way he is going to be my husband, so I will overlook that he is starting to drink every day. (me) Well I'm tired are you ready for bed? No, you go ahead (do he know I want to lay down with him?) Now he is Controlling when and where I get it! Do he know that's what a husband supposed to do? (lay down per my request!) Do he know that's part of why he is here? I think we need a talk before this marriage takes place. Months later..........(him) Hey I'm gone! Where are you going? I will be back! (HUH)? He leaves. I don't like that, when he says I'll be back and don't tell me where he is going. Is that what men do? Or Seagrams or another Spirit I know nothing about? You know he is being very inconsiderate lately and selfish! And this is before the wedding. (NOT NOW GOD ICAN'T HEAR MYSELF THINK!) You know these things are minor to some people, but he put a ring on it!(I didn't know he thought that was all he was supposed to do.) That's all I wanted was ring and not a husband. The door opens, hey... (me) hey....It's late, Yeah, I was drinking with REMY. Oh he told me to tell you hi. So he staggering at the moment. (me) You know this is not working out, you are drunk almost every day, for some reason I don't trust you or your judgment and I can't put my life and my kids life in danger. SO you need to leave! Go stay with REMY, because he gets more of your time than me! So he packs up and leave, I kept the ring (I may have paid for it in the long run anyway). Months later...... I know I did the right thing, but why am I so sad? I spent a lot of money on this dude, enabling his bad behavior. I haven't had a drink in four years, let me get some wine (that's low calorie right?), I'll take two (I'm at the liquor store). I'm back home......this wine is tasty why did I stop drinking you? YYEESS! Alone at last, let me cook something to eat. Is this a pattern? I don't know (GOD, I'M NOT READY TO TALK TO YOU, YOU ARE PROBABLY MAD AT ME?) I can handle this Loneliness and Abandonment.(friend) Hey girl where have you been? I haven't seen you in Church, oh I been going through some things (BEER), but I'm fine. Months later..............I'm going to have to move, I'm in so much Debt, from Seagrams, I can't even afford my BEER and Takeout. Well kids were moving, to better schools (Yeah right!) I mean where mommy can afford her drinks. Hey, maybe I'll find love out there, in a new neighborhood!

Chapter 8

GREYGOOSE

Moving day...............Hi(me), Do you need help moving your furniture? (me)Yes! I didn't know who was going to move me? (me) What's your name? Macadamia Nut. What's your name? They call me Greygoose. It seems to change very often. I like to Conform with the Times. (me) Well I don't have much money to pay you, that's okay, I don't have nothing to offer you but a nut (he didn't say that.) LET THE GAMES BEGIN! Now I know I do not want a relationship with him(I wish he just come over from time to time and give me what he has to offer (other than that we have nothing, but two hurting people in the world). Well it's Friday night, let me get started on my 30 pack of BEER, let me call this nut for him to come over and feed me some LIES. (If I drink enough I can't hear him anyway) (NOT NOW GOD, I KNOW WHAT I'M DOING!) SSSOOOO......he comes over, (me) You know what? I haven't a cycle this month. (I'm thinking early menopause YES!). Well I'm going to get a pregnancy test, I'll be right back! He is crazy, I can't be pregnant with him? No can't be! LORD IS THIS A JOKE OF YOURS, THAT'S NOT FUNNY! LORD I DON'T LOVE HIM I DON'T LOVE MYSELF, WELL I KNOW I WON';T BE DRINKING WITH THIS LITTLE ONE IN MY BELLY! Okay, Okay I will stop crying, but you can go now, you did enough damage (me). (Hey I have to blame someone right!). Ten months later.............She is beautiful! (me) Do he have to come over and see his child, I don't want him to start feeding her LIES and DECEPTION. You know what? These men are going to be the DEATH of ME! Why do I keep ATRACTING the same type of man? Do I love FOOD so much!? Or is it the COMFORT of whatever SPIRIT I take on.

Chapter 9
I MEET ALLWAYS!

WHY DON'T YOU GIVE UP DRINKING FOR FORTY DAYS. (ME) GOD IS THAT YOU, BECAUSE I DON'T WANT TO GIVE THAT UP, SO I KNOW IT'S YOU AND IT'S A GOOD IDEA. I'LL TRY, ARE YOU GOING TO HOLD MY HAND? ALLWAYS......MONTHS LATER....I'M BEEN REALLY FEELING GOOD WITHOUT DRINKING AND OVEREATINGAND NOW LITTLE LOVE IS WALKING AROUND KNOWING WHAT LOVE IS AND WHO LOVE IS. HAVE SHE BEEN INSIDE ME THE WHOLE TIME? GOD CAN I CALL YOU MY ALLWAYS? I KNOW PEOPLE HAVE SO MANY NAMES FOR YOU, BECAUSE YOU ARE A LOT TO A LOT OF PEOPLE. THANK YOU FOR SAVING ME FROM FLESH EATING SPIRITS. NOW I'M EATING NOTHING BUT THE TRUE BREAD AND DRINKING FROM YOUR CUP. I DID NOT KNOW THAT LOVE IS HELPING ME LOSE WEIGHT. ALL THIS TIME I'VE BEEN LOCKED UP, BUT LOVE RELEASED ME........

Chapter 10

NOW I'M ADDICTED TO ALWAYS.

THE BEGINNING

www.ingramcontent.com/pod-product-compliance
Ingram Content Group UK Ltd.
Pitfield, Milton Keynes, MK11 3LW, UK
UKHW022217230426
12048UKWH00016BA/910